THE TASTE OF TESO

A culinary tour of our culture

Beatrice Okwalinga

ISBN: Softcover   978-1-5434-9452-5
        Hardcover   978-1-5434-9453-2
        EBook   978-1-5434-9454-9

Print information available on the last page

Rev. date: 03/01/2019

To order additional copies of this book, contact:
Xlibris
0800-056-3182
www.xlibrispublishing.co.uk
Orders@ Xlibrispublishing.co.uk

Dedication

In memory of my late, dear parents, Samwiri and Isabella Amucu Aisu, who taught us to share and to value, love and appreciate our rich Iteso Culture.

Acknowledgements

If it takes a village to raise a child, it takes more than one village to write a cookbook!

I thank my husband, Michael Okwalinga-Emokol, UK family and friends for their encouragement, patience and support; Uganda family: Rebecca Okiring, Toto Loyce Otai, Tata Naume Apolot, Christine, Alvin, Adeline, William, Emma and others who helped make the cookbook better; Toto Akaliait Agnes Osuban, the Secretariat, Iteso Cultural Union UK and the Iteso community, for encouraging me; the Editorial and technical team: Helena Okiring, Isabella Arionget, Beatrice Aide, Francis Oliso and Caroline Agiru, without whom this cookbook would just be pie in the sky.

As much as possible, this cook book seeks to take you through a culinary tour of Teso, giving you the opportunity to recreate both staple and more contemporary dishes to suit your taste. It is a tribute to the previous generations of women and our legacy to the next generation of bold food lovers who love Teso, upon whom the duty to continue the custom of healthy, distinctive dining rests.

Food from Teso region is very lean, in the sense that it is prepared simply, to conserve as much of the natural flavour and nutrients as possible. Most of the foods are boiled or slow cooked, and roasting is done over hot coals. Food is preserved by sun drying or smoking on the fire. Frying of food was a foreign concept.

It is important to remember that in a typical Teso kitchen, ingredients are not weighed or measured. They are simply added, depending on how much food is being cooked; this in turn depends on the numbers one is cooking for. If you ever asked how much of an ingredient you needed to use, or how long you should cook the food for, you would always be told to use your eyes, smell and taste the food and you would know in your heart. This is the same with the timing, hence the saying that Ateso women cook from their hearts. The measurements and timings I have given in the book are more of a guide and, when trying to recreate the recipe, you should, as much as possible, cook from your heart!

Wherever possible, I have given the scientific or botanical name of the dish, as well as its Ateso and Kumam names.

Traditional ingredients commonly used in a typical Teso kitchen.

Throughout our journey, you will find references to natural seasonings, additives and herbs. They give our food a distinct, rich flavour while enhancing its nutritious value for maximum health benefits.

Liquid Soda ash– (Abalang)

Found in a typical Teso kitchen is an ingredient called 'abalang' which is local salt and tenderiser. This ingredient is widely used in the preparation of most traditional dishes as a tenderiser and as a salt, giving them a certain distinctive taste.

'Abalang', which is in form of ash, is made by burning certain plants, usually dry cotton stems, mixed with other plants like the amaranths which contain flowers and thorns, or dried banana peelings to produce ash which is very rich in minerals. The ash is then distilled by placing it in a porous pot (my mother always insisted on this) or a container with holes at the bottom. A mesh cloth or sieve is placed at the bottom of the pot to stop the ash particles from going through. This is placed on top of a receptor dish for collecting the liquid; water is added to the ash and the result is a brown coloured liquid called 'abalang'. It is like having a chemistry lab in a kitchen.

In today's kitchen, the substitute for liquid soda ash is sodium bicarbonate and rock salt, also known as 'amagadi'.

My father (RIP) used to tell us that the reason certain illnesses like heart disease and high blood pressure were rare in Teso was because they consumed abalang in most of their foods. It is said to have medicinal properties that help with high blood pressure, heart condition, and it acts as an anti-oxidant.

Ghee – (Akinyet na'ituk)

Ghee is widely eaten in Teso. The oil comes from processing milk, which is churned to separate the milk from the fat. The fat is cooked to produce pure ghee.

I vividly remember the times we used to go to spend holidays with our maternal grandmother (RIP). Very early the next day, without fail, you woke up to a gourd tied to a post with a rope which you used to rock. This was the churning process used to separate the milk from the fat. You ended up with sour milk and finally ghee. This was one of the skills you were taught at a very early age. I remember being terrified at the thought of the gourd hitting the post and shuttering with all its contents! Luckily, that never happened.

Using a special process, the raw fat is removed from the gourd and boiled in a saucepan to turn it into ghee. This is used as a food enhancer in sauces such as cow pea sauce,'emagira', added to foods like 'matooke' and cassava. Traditionally, foods were not fried but oils such as ghee and shea butter were added to enhance the flavour. The ghee can also be added to groundnut paste to form what is locally known as 'emuna'. Delicious with millet bread or just on its own.

Shea Butter (*Butyrospermum parkii*) – 'Akungurut'

Shea butter is extracted from seeds of the African shea tree commonly known as *'ekungur'* in Teso. Shea butter is used to add flavour to dishes and can also be eaten as a spread. It is also very good for the skin and you can find it being used as a dry skin remedy. The tree is grown in most parts of Teso and apart from the shea butter, the wood is also used for building and curving stools. It is also known to produce high-quality charcoal.

The processed product is sold in most local markets.

Tamarind (*Tamarindus indicus*) – '*Apedur / Cwaya*'

Tamarind comes from a tropical tree that is found growing in most parts of Teso. Its pulpy seeds are used for many things but in Teso, the juices are extracted and used as flavour enhancers for foods like millet porridge and millet bread. It can also be taken as a drink or used as a salad dressing or dip.

Tamarind provides energy and sugar together with essential nutrients such as potassium, phosphorus, magnesium, calcium and vitamin C. It also contains a number of organic compounds that make it a powerful antioxidant and anti-inflammatory agent. (1)

Leafy Okra (*Abelmoschus esculentus*) – 'Alilot'

This is a leafy vegetable crop found in most parts of Teso and it is added to sauces to give a mucilaginous consistency after cooking. The extract from the fruit is often added to different recipes like stews and sauces to increase the consistency. Okra mucilage has medicinal applications when used as a plasma replacement or blood volume expander. The mucilage of okra binds cholesterol and bile acid carrying toxins dumped into it by the liver. (2) It forms a main ingredient when preparing 'eboo' but can be added to many dishes like 'emagira', meats or eaten on its own.

Okra is rich in fibre, carbohydrate, folate, protein, Vitamins A & C, magnesium.

Contents

Muskmelon (Cucumis melo) – 'Akobokob / Okwerkwer' 1

Black-eyed Peas (*Vigna unguiculata*) – '*Imare / Ngor*' 3

Black-eyed pea stew plain – 'Edek / Emagira' 4

Black-eyed peas with Sweet Potatoes – '*Emangor*' 6

Black-eyed pea curry 7

Beans - '*Emaroge*' 8

Black-eyed pea leaves in peanut butter sauce – '*Eboo /Ebou*' 10

Dried pea leaves – Dried '*Eboo / ebou*' 12

Cloeme (*Gynandropsis qynandra*) – '*Ecadoi / Ecaboi / Akeu*' 13

Balanite tree (*Balanites aegyptiaca*) – '*Ecomai*' 15

Amaranth – '*Eboga*' 16

Hibiscus (*Hibiscus sabdariffa*) – '*Emalakang / Amalakwang*' 18

Pumpkin (*Cucurbita pepo*) – '*Asujo / Esujo*' 19

Pumpkin Leaves 20

Steamed or boiled Pumpkin 20

Mushrooms – "Ebaale" 21

Imaruk 22

Eswei 24

White Ants – 'Ikong' 25

Groundnuts (Arachis hypogoea) –' Emaido / Emado' 27

Roasted Groundnuts 29

Groundnut Sauce – 'Epila / Epilili' 30

Groundnut Curry sauce..30

Steamed Groundnut sauce in banana leaves...31

Boiled Groundnuts 32

Sesame seeds (Seasamum indicum) – 'Ikanyum / Nino' 33

Sesame balls 33

Bambara Nuts (Vigna subterranean) – 'Isuk' 34

Fish – 'Agaria' 35

Smoked Fish in groundnut sauce – Traditional version 36

Smoked Fish in groundnut stew – Modern version 37

Fresh Steamed Fish 38

Steamed fish in banana leaves 39

Silver fish (Rastrineobola argentea) – 'Aiyoi / Onang' 40

Fried Fish 42

Meat – Akiring 43

Smoked meat in groundnut sauce – Traditional Version 43

Smoked meat in groundnut sauce – Modern Version 44

Boiled meat. 46

Beef Stew. 47

Roast Meat. 48

Cow Foot – 'Emolokony' 48

Oxtail 50

Abdominal Offal – 'Amoeteka' 50

Chicken – 'Akokor' 51

Egg in groundnut Sauce 51

Boiled Chicken 52

Smoked Chicken in groundnut sauce 53

BBQ Style Roast Chicken legs 54

Finger Millet (Eleusine coracana) – 'Alos / Kal' 55

Millet Bread – 'Atap' 56

Millet porridge – "Akima" 57

Sorghum (Sorghum bicolor) – 'Imumwa / Bel' 58

Cassava (Manihot esculenta) – 'Emuogo' 59

Boiled Cassava 60

Boiled mashed Cassava 61

Cassava Chips 61

Cassava pancakes – 'Ecokil' 62

Yams (Dioscorea alata) – "Abatot" 63

Sweet Potatoes (Ipomoea batatas) – 'Acok / Kata' 64

Boiled Sweet Potatoes 65

Clay baked potatoes – 'Emukaro' 66

Dried sliced potatoes – 'Amukeke' 67

Sweet Potato chips – Oven baked 67

Maize – 'Ekirididi' 68

Grilled/Roasted Maize 69

Boiled Maize 70

Maize meal (Posho) – "Euga" 70

Green Bananas / Plantain – 'Etaget' 71

Rice – 'Emuceri' 72

Pilau Rice 73

Doughnuts – 'Mandazi' 75

Chapati 76

Millet Brew – 'Ajon' 77

Muskmelon (Cucumis melo) – 'Akobokob / Okwerkwer'

Muskmelon is a yellow bulb-like crawling plant grown in most parts of Teso. It is quite similar to water melon but smaller and takes about four months to mature. Muskmelon can be planted with other crops such as millet and potatoes. The pods are crushed to get rid of the seeds, which are preserved and then dried under the sun.

Mary Natuk, a mother of seven and resident of Lotome Sub County in Napak District, says, "A family without muskmelon or cacabus during dry season is not a safe family because this is the only vegetable that guarantees that children will drink water throughout the day," (3)

Preparation Time: 1 hour

Cooking Time: 1 hour

Serves: 4

This Muskmelon recipe is an ode to a classic favourite loved by all. Delicious with groundnut sauce.

Ingredients:

250g dried Muskmelon (*Akobokob*)

3 tbsp. Liquid soda ash *'abalang'* or 25g if using rock salt *'amagadi'*

½ tsp Salt to taste

6 tbsp smooth peanut butter

Preparation:

1. Soak the dried muskmelon in cold water for 1 hr.
2. Wash the muskmelon making sure you remove any soil and gently wash the inner part which contains flesh / pulp.
3. Add water to a large pan and bring to boil
4. Add muskmelon in the boiling water and leave to cook for 30 mins or until slightly tender.
5. Add liquid soda ash and salt to taste.[1]
6. Leave to simmer for another 10 minutes until muskmelon is soft and tender.
7. Add peanut butter and mix to a semi thick consistency; if too thick, add a little water.
8. Remove from fire.
9. Best eaten with millet bread (*Atap*) or Sweet potatoes.

Variation:

Cooked muskmelon can be added to other dishes such as smoked meats in ground nut sauce, fish, chicken or any leafy vegetables.

Storage and Preservation:

- Cooked, cooled muskmelon *without* peanut butter can be put in a container and frozen.
- When required, remove from freezer and defrost overnight. Heat and add peanut butter or add to smoked meat if you prefer.

---

1 Adding the liquid soda ash too early will make the muskmelon mushy.

Black-eyed Peas (*Vigna unguiculata*) – 'Imare / Ngor'

These are legume seeds that are grown widely in Teso. They are simple to prepare and can be served in various forms such as soup, broth and can be added to salads or casseroles. Black-eyed peas offer many health benefits and are packed with a lot of essential nutrients, such as fibre which helps with a healthy digestive system, iron which prevents anaemia, zinc to help reduce the risk of macular degeneration. Peas are also high in protein and are a good source of magnesium and potassium which can help to lower the risk of heart disease (4). Peas are packed with so many nutrients, no wonder it is one of the main foods served almost daily in most houses.

Black-eyed pea stew plain – 'Edek / Emagira'

Cooking Time: 1 hour

Serves: 4

A tasty stew made from dried, crushed and winnowed black-eyed peas. The process of winnowing is done traditionally using a special tray; done in the wind which blows away the husks and black eyes. Alternatively, you can buy the already crushed peas from any African food store. Enjoy with boiled rice, maize or millet bread.

Ingredients:

250g crushed black-eyed peas

3 tbsp. liquid soda ash *'abalang'* or 25g rock salt *'amagadi'*

½ tsp Salt

3 tbsp. Ghee

2 tbsp. peanut butter (optional)

Method

1. Clean the crushed peas and soak in cold water.
2. Wash the peas and add to a pan of water. Add liquid soda ash to the mixture and bring to boil.
3. Keep removing the scum like residue which consists of the peas' covers and the black eye bits and keep stirring. When the entire residue is removed, reduce the heat to a simmer. Keep stirring until the sauce turns to a thick consistency. *(The Iteso use a special wooden stick for stirring the sauce).* Add salt to taste.
4. Add peanut butter (optional).
5. Remove from the heat and add ghee.
6. Serve with millet bread, sweet potatoes.

Variations:

1. Add cow pea leaves to the sauce after the entire residue is removed.
2. Add peanut butter and ghee.
3. Use split yellow or red lentils as an alternative to the black-eyed peas.

Black-eyed peas with Sweet Potatoes – *'Emangor'*

Preparation Time: 1 hour

Cooking Time: 45 mins

Serves: 4

This is a delightful mix of mashed sweet potato and fresh black-eyed peas. A tasty take to comfort food, enjoyed in the harvest season. This dish is loved by children and adults alike, usually as a midday meal served after people return from a hard day's work in the gardens.

Ingredients

300g freshly picked black-eyed peas

6 medium sized sweet potatoes, peeled and diced into cubes

Salt to taste

Method.

To *make the peas*

1. Wash the fresh peas and add to a pot of boiling water.
2. Bring to boil and reduce the heat to a simmer, add salt and any other seasoning required; stir regularly until soft to the touch.
3. Remove the heat and put to the side.

To *make the sweet potatoes*

1. In a separate pot, wash the diced potatoes, add to a pot of water; just enough to cover the potatoes, and boil until the potatoes are soft and tender.
2. Drain any water from the potatoes. Add the peas to the pot of potatoes and mingle / mash into a soft paste.
3. Serve immediately. Can be eaten on its own or with a peanut sauce – *'epiila'*.

Variation:

- Use fresh beans or Bambara nuts as an alternative to the fresh black-eyed peas.
- If using dried legumes, remember to soak them in cold water for 1 hour before cooking.

Storage:

The dish can be cooled and eaten cold. Delicious as an afternoon snack with a cup of tea.

Black-eyed pea curry

Preparation Time: 1 hour

Cooking Time: 1 hour

Serves: 4

Ingredients:

250g dried black eyed peas

2 cloves of garlic

1 medium red onion

1 can coconut milk (optional)

1 tsp cumin seeds

1/2 tsp mustard seed

1 tsp turmeric

1 tsp garam masala

Method:

1. Pick through the peas, rinse thoroughly and soak in cold water for 1 hour.
2. Put in a pot and cover with water. Add salt to taste. Bring to boil, and reduce to a simmer. Cook the peas until soft (40-45 minutes).Check the peas to make sure they are soft to the touch. Drain.
3. While the peas are cooking, prepare the coconut sauce.
4. Heat oil in the pan, add cumin seeds and stir for 2 mins.
5. Reduce heat; add onions, garlic and ginger. Keep turning until the onions are golden and tender. Add the rest of the spices and stir until the aroma is given off.
6. Add tomatoes and keep stirring until it turns into a thick paste. Add the peas, coconut milk (if using or else add water) and salt to taste. Simmer gently until the consistency reaches the required level.
7. Sprinkle the parsley to garnish and serve with rice.

Variation:

For the recipe above, use pigeon peas, chickpeas, beans or lentils as a substitute.

Beans[2] - 'Emaroge'

Beans are legume seeds widely grown and eaten in Teso. As it is quick maturing, it forms part of the everyday diet for many families and is commonly used to feed in established institutions such as schools, hospitals, prisons etc. Beans also became a common dish during the famine periods as it was one of the many foods distributed by The World Food Program. Beans are a good source of protein and carbohydrates and are known for their antioxidant properties. Beans can be cooked and eaten in their fresh state as a sauce and an accompaniment to any staple dishes such as rice, posho, millet bread, and matooke.

Beans are dried as a way to preserve them and they can be cooked in the dried state as well.

One of the recipes that reminds me of home is posho and beans or rice and beans.

To *prepare bean sauce:*

Ingredients

250g of beans

1 medium onion

2 carrots

3 large tomatoes (chopped)

2 cloves of garlic

1 tsp. mixed spice

½ tsp. ground ginger powder

1tsp. paprika

1tsp. curry powder

1 Maggi cube / or 2 tbsp. Royco mix

1 eggplant (optional)

2 tbsp. olive oil

½ tsp. black coarse pepper

1 tbsp. ghee

½ tsp salt – add if more is required

---

2 Use beans as a substitute for all the black-eyed pea recipes

Method:

1. If using dried beans, sort, wash and soak overnight.
2. Add water in a pan and bring to boil.
3. Rinse the beans and add to the pan, add water so it covers the beans by a couple of inches, bring it to boil and reduce the heat so the beans simmer slowly for 45 mins.
4. Turn the beans and check to see if they are soft. Add the salt. Let the beans simmer till you need to use them in the next stage.
5. In a separate pan, add the oil, fry the onions until they are golden brown.
6. Add the garlic, and the rest of the spices. Add the chopped tomatoes and the rest of the vegetables and cook till they are soft.
7. Make sure the beans are cooked before you add them to the sauce. Mix the Royco or Maggi cube with water and add to the bean sauce. Let it cook for another 5 mins.
8. Remove from the fire. Add ghee before serving.
9. Delicious with boiled rice or maize meal.

Variations:

- Add peanut butter in the last 5 mins of cooking.
- Use coconut milk instead of water and add to the beans after frying.

Black-eyed pea leaves in peanut butter sauce – 'Eboo / Ebou'

Cooking Time: 30 mins

Serves: 4

A rich vegetable sauce made with fresh cow-pea and okra leaves cooked in ground nut sauce. Pea leaves provide roughage for digestion, is known to be good for eyesight and is rich in vitamin B and E complex. An absolute delight when served with millet bread or posho, potatoes and rice.

Ingredients:

500g freshly picked pea leaves

50g leafy okra (ladies' fingers)

3 tbsp. liquid soda ash, '*abalang*' or 25g rock salt '*amagadi*'

Freshly picked mushrooms (optional)

½ tsp Salt

6 tbsp. smooth peanut butter

Preparation:

1. Separate the leaves from the stalks.
2. Spread the fresh leaves under the sun for 10 mins to wither the leaves slightly and to get rid of any pests.
3. Add water to a pot and bring to boil.
4. Add the liquid soda ash.
5. Wash the okra leaves and add to the pan.
6. Wash the fresh leaves thoroughly to remove any soil.
7. Add the leaves to the pan, add salt and cook for 25 minutes or until the leaves are soft and tender.
8. Add peanut butter and cook for 3 minutes
9. Remove from fire.
10. Serve with any of the following staple foods; millet bread, sweet potatoes, *matooke or posho.*

Variations:

1. Fresh diced mushrooms can be added during cooking, after adding the leaves but before adding peanut paste.
2. If using dried mushrooms, remember to soak them first for 30 mins, wash before adding during cooking.

Storage and preservation:

- The fresh leaves can be dried under the sun as a way of preserving to be used later.
- Cooked cooled eboo sauce **without** peanut butter can be put in a container and frozen.
- When required, remove from the freezer and defrost overnight. Heat and add peanut butter.

Dried pea leaves – Dried *'Eboo / ebou'*

A different but equally delightful variation to this staple dish. Eboo cooked with fully withered, sun-dried leaves is enjoyed in the summer or dry season, when fresh leaves are out of season. This method is also a preservation technique. The leaves are soaked in cold water for 30 mins before cooking. Follow the process above to give you a near fresh dish of Eboo.

Dried pea leaves powder – 'Einyongole'

Ingredients:

300g Dried eboo leaves[3]

2 tbsp. liquid soda ash *'abalang'* or 2g rock salt *'amagadi'*

½ tsp salt

6 tbsp. Peanut butter

1tbsp. ghee

Method:

1. Crush the dried leaves into a powder or use a motor and pestle to pound the leaves.
2. Add water to a pot and bring to boil.
3. Add liquid soda ash and salt.
4. Add the crushed powder into the boiling water and keep stirring for 5 mins.
5. Reduce the heat to a simmer for another 3 mins, until the sauce is cooked.
6. Add peanut butter.
7. Add ghee (optional).
8. Best eaten with sweet potatoes, millet bread or matooke.

---

3 Put the dried leaves out in the sun to make sure they are completely dry or use the oven.

Cloeme (*Gynandropsis qynandra*) – '*Ecadoi / Ecaboi / Akeu*'

Preparation Time: 30 mins

Cooking Time: 1 hour

Serves: 6

Cloeme is a delicious dish made from a combination of leafy vegetable plants of the amaranths family also known as spiderplant. The stalks, leaves and flowers from this plant make up what is called '*ecadoi*' dish.

It is a delicacy from Teso and the dish is served during important celebrations such as marriage, celebrating new harvest, but it also forms part of the main dishes for most families. It is rich in vitamin A, vitamin C, folate, calcium, iron, potassium, and protein.

Ingredients

750g cleome – *ecadoi / ecaboi*

500g bundles amaranths – *'eboga'*

100g *Cissus adenocaulis* – *'Emoros'* leaves

1 cup sour milk or 1 lemon[4] – Or more depending on how sour you want the dish to taste.

325g Peanut butter

Salt (optional)

Method:

1. Spread the leaves out in the sun for 5 minutes.
2. Gather the leaves, shake them to remove any soil and pests.
3. Place in bundles and finely chop the leaves with the stalks and flowers if any.
4. Chop the *'eboga'* leaves and put aside.
5. Wash the vegetables thoroughly to remove any soil.
6. Place in a pot of boiling water (use a clay pot for best results).
7. Keep turning until the leaves are almost cooked.
8. Wash the *'eboga'* thoroughly and add to the pot. Cook until soft. Remove from the fire and put aside.
9. Prepare *'emoros'* leaves, wash and add to the pot containing the *'ecadoi'* and *'eboga'*.

10. Bring to boil and cook until *'emoros'* is cooked.
11. Remove from the fire, add sour milk (or lemon juice if using) and leave till the next day for added taste otherwise, leave for 2 – 3 hours.
12. When required, scoop the required amount from the pot, heat it up, add peanut butter and salt (optional).
13. Serve with millet bread, delicious!

Variations:

- Use lemon juice or Greek yogurt as a substitute for sour milk.
- Use *'Calaloo'* as an alternative to cleome.
- It was common to leave the cooked cleome mixed with sour milk in the pot for 2 – 3 days. When required, scoop the required quantity, heat it up and add peanut butter. The flavour and taste is to die for!
- This dish tastes even better when eaten the next day.

_____
4 Tip by Beatrice Aide

Balanite tree (*Balanites aegyptiaca*) – '*Ecomai*'

Preparation Time: 30 mins

Cooking Time: 1 hour

Serves: 4

Balanite dish comes from the young leaves and shoots of the balanite tree, also known as the desert date.

The young leaves and shoots are a rich source of protein, providing an excellent vegetable, especially during the dry season. Balanite tree is drought resistant and grows in most parts of Teso.

Ingredients

250g leaves and shoots from the balanite tree

1 cup Sour milk (Substitute 1 lemon or Greek yogurt)

300g Peanut butter

Salt (optional)

Method:

1. Cut the branch of the balanite tree and pick off the leaves and shoots.
2. Wash the leaves and add to a pot of boiling water. The water should just cover the leaves.
3. Bring to boil and reduce to simmer, keep stirring until the leaves are soft and tender.
4. Leave to cool and strain out all the liquid from the leaves.
5. Pound to a paste using a pestle and motor (or use a blender).
6. Put paste in a pot and add sour milk and leave to stand for up to 3 days if required (optional).
7. Scoop the required quantity, add to a pan, and add peanut butter. Bring to boil.
8. Delicious with millet bread or sweet potatoes.

Amaranth – 'Eboga'

Preparation Time: 15 mins

Cooking Time: 30 mins

Serves: 4

'Eboga' is from the amaranth plant family; a tasty edible species cultivated in many parts of the world as part of the local diet. It's quite common in Teso cuisine and usually served on a bed of rice as an accompaniment to main proteins like beans or meat. 'Eboga' is extremely nutritious containing vitamin A, vitamin C, folate, calcium, iron, potassium, and protein. Amaranth can be found growing wild around the homes and is easily available all year round.

There are many ways of preparing 'eboga'; the simplest being steaming or simply boiling it and eating it as a side dish or as a soup. One of my favourites is a recipe below.

Ingredients:

4 bundles *'Eboga'* leaves

1 medium onion, diced

1 large tomato chopped

Green, red, and yellow sweet peppers thinly sliced

Olive oil

Salt, paprika, curry powder, black pepper to season

Peanut butter (optional)

Method:

1. Wash the *'eboga'* and shake off any water. Chop both the stalks and leaves to required size.
2. Heat the olive oil in a pan, add the onions and stir until golden brown.
3. Add the seasoning and stir for 2 mins.
4. Add the tomato, then the peppers.
5. Add the *'eboga'* and cook for 3-5 minutes.
6. Serve as a side dish in meats or beans; it can also be served with rice, *posho* or *matooke*.

Variations:

- Add peanut butter to cooked *'eboga'* to give you a delicious dish of *'eboga'* in peanut sauce.
- Use Spinach or collard or kale greens as an alternative to *'eboga'* leaves.

Spinach in peanut butter is a delicious dish loved by all who have tasted it. To prepare spinach in peanut butter, follow the recipe above for amaranths. Use frozen spinach to get the same results.

Hibiscus (*Hibiscus sabdariffa*) – 'Emalakang / Amalakwang'

Cooking Time: 1 hour

The plant is cultivated in some parts of Teso and its leaves form one of the main dishes prepared and consumed in most households. The dish is said to be beneficial to breast feeding mothers as it helps in the production of milk. It is also said to act as an appetiser for patients with low appetite.

The leaves of this plant have a distinct sour taste and their preparation may vary according to individual taste.

Ingredients:

500g Hibiscus leaves

Peanut butter

Salt

If using fresh hibiscus leaves:

1. Bring a pot of water to boil.
2. Wash the leaves thoroughly to remove any soil and add to the pot of boiling water.
3. The cooking process causes the green colouring to be released. Cook until tender.
4. Once cooked, the leaves will turn a pale green colour. Drain the water from the leaves completely and keep a little aside for later use if required.
5. Pound the leaves or use a blender to make a paste.
6. Add groundnut paste and mix to the required consistency. If preferred, use some of the drained water to mix with the groundnut paste. This will give an enhanced sour taste akin to the taste of sour milk.
7. Cook for another 2 – 3 mins. Delicious with sweet potatoes.

Variations:

- When using dry hibiscus, remember to soak in water for at least 1 hour before cooking. Use the process above. Instead of pounding or blending the cooked leaves, they can be crushed before soaking.

Tip:[5] Using 1 tbsp. of olive oil, fry finely chopped onions until golden brown, add the hibiscus sauce, cook for 2 mins and then add peanut butter, delicious.

---

5 By Damalie Oluka

Pumpkin (*Cucurbita pepo*) – 'Asujo / Esujo'

Traditionally, pumpkin plants could be found growing in the backyard of every homestead and they provided a simple meal for most families. Today, pumpkins are grown for their commercial value. Pumpkins are similar to butternut squash but they are round with smooth skin and the flesh is a deep yellow to orange colour. The inside contains pulp and the seeds which are edible when dried and fried or roasted.

Pumpkin Leaves

The leaves of pumpkin provide very tasty vegetables when steamed or boiled.

To *prepare pumpkin vegetables:*

1. Pick the leaves; remove the hairy bits on the surface of the stalk and leaf. This is done by carefully peeling off the skin from the stalk to the leaf.
2. Put the leaves in the sun to wither slightly and to get rid of any pests.
3. Shake off any soil and shred or chop the leaves.
4. Wash the leaves and steam or boil them in salted water. Add onions, tomatoes and curry powder.
5. Eat with sweet potatoes or *'matooke'*.

Variations:

- The leaves can also be cooked with peanut butter and eaten with *'matooke'*, *posho* or sweet potatoes.
- Fry onions, add curry powder, tomatoes and the pumpkin leaves.

Steamed or boiled Pumpkin.

1. Cut open the pumpkin and scoop out the pulp with the seeds.
2. Slice the pumpkin into pieces.
3. Steam or boil with the skin. Pumpkin can also be roasted with the skin on.
4. When ready, eat as a snack or serve as a side dish.

Variations:

- Dried Pumpkin seeds can be fried or roasted to provide a nutritious snack.
- Make pumpkin soup by boiling the pumpkin, remove the skin and mash or blend the pumpkin. Add water and season as required.

Mushrooms – "*Ebaale*"

A common feature of all the mushrooms eaten in Teso is that they grow wildly by anti-hills and also gardens especially those planted with millet. The mushrooms will usually appear after the white ants season.

They are delicious and easy to prepare.

These are the types of mushroom found mainly in Teso.

- *Imaruk* – giant umbrella like cups
- *Eswei* – grow in white mass clusters
- *Itimi jako* – known for their black colour
- *Akou Atitip*

The mushrooms can be eaten fresh or can be dried for later use. They can also be served as a main sauce, used as an accompaniment to other dishes or added to many dishes, such as the leafy vegetable dishes, dried meats and they are delicious in peanut butter sauce or sesame.

Imaruk

These are known locally as giant mushrooms because of their large umbrella like heads. These mushrooms will sprout and grow to a giant size within a very short time, usually 24 hours and will perish within a very short time. They are found growing from certain anthills known locally as *'akwaresia'* meaning the anthills from which the flying ants come out in the night.

The mushrooms are picked and usually left to dry under the sun. However, they can be cooked in their fresh state as a simple mushroom soup dish or added to other sauces.

Method – dried mushrooms

1. Soak the dried mushrooms in water.
2. Heat water in a pan and add liquid soda ash *'abalang'*.
3. Wash the mushrooms and add them to the boiling water.
4. Reduce the heat and cook until soft and tender.
5. Stir in the peanut butter to a required consistency. If too thick, add water.
6. Serve hot with millet bread or sweet potatoes.

Variations:

The mushrooms can be added to other sauces like smoked meat or greens, to make a delicious dish.

Eswei

Eswei is found growing around anthills and they will normally germinate following the white ants season. They grow in clusters of small white masses. This type of mushroom is prepared as a delicacy during certain traditional ceremonies such as eating new millet and marriage ceremonies.

Because they grow too close to the soil, the mushrooms require careful handling and preparation to remove the soil. Once picked, the mushrooms are put out in the sun to dry.

Method of preparation is similar for all types of mushrooms. It is distinct for its pleasant aroma when cooked. Delicious in ground nut sauce.

White Ants – 'Ikong'

The Iteso were eating these insects as part of their protein diet long before the scientists started worrying about the effects of methane gas on the environment. White ants are flying insects that come out of anthills.

There is a particular season for white ants. To collect the ants, holes are dug around the anthill so that the white ants crawl into them and can't get out. They are collected from the holes and taken to be prepared. The ants that fly away are attracted to light or lamps. It is common to find groups of children seated around a lamp with a white sheet on the ground catching the ants.

There is a different species of white ants that is trapped using a very clever method. Using clay, tunnel pipes are built from the hole where the ants will be flying out of to a pot which is covered with leaves. A group of young boys or men beat sticks together to a certain tune, to entice the ants out of the anthill. Like lambs to the slaughter, the ants will make their way through the clay tunnel into the pots. These ants are known as *'emome'* in Ateso.

Once captured, the ants are fried in a pan to kill them. They are then spread out in the sun to dry. The wings are removed by rubbing the ants gently together and then separated using a winnower. The ants can be eaten straight away or they are washed, salted and roasted to give you a delicious snack of insects.

The insects can also be pounded together with roasted groundnuts or simsim using a mortar and pestle or a blender to give you a smooth paste known locally as *'emuna'*. This is eaten with millet bread, or can be used as a spread on foods like cassava, bread or sweet potatoes..

Groundnuts (*Arachis hypogoea*) –' *Emaido / Emado*'

Groundnuts are a popular snack and an important part of the diet in Teso. There are many varieties of groundnuts grown throughout the region. The picture shows the red variety.

Groundnuts are eaten in a variety of ways: raw, roasted, boiled, mixed with sesame seeds and made into a *groundnut butter*, ground into a powder, or cooked into a thick savoury sauce. Groundnut sauce is delicious and can be eaten with any meal, over *"matooke"*, sweet potatoes or rice; or stewed with legumes, leaf vegetables, fish and meats.

Groundnuts are a delicious, healthy nutritious snack that contains a great deal of protein, fibre, calcium, potassium and iron, oil and energy.

Groundnut paste forms the main part of most traditional dishes served in Teso. It is widely used as an accompaniment to dishes, an enhancer or a base of a dish and in most cases can also be consumed on its own as a sauce. Groundnut paste is also used as a spread or dip on foods like cassava, sweet potatoes and bread.

Traditionally, to make the ground nut paste, the dry nuts are shelled, cleaned and dry roasted. When cooled, the covers or husks are removed from the nuts and pounded using a pestle and mortar until it is in form of a paste. In the old days, a grinding stone would be used to grind the paste to a smooth consistency used for making sauces. These days, technology allows for the whole process from shelling to grinding to be done using special grinding machines.

Roasted Groundnuts

500g of shelled groundnuts

Salt to taste

Cooking Time: 25 mins

Method:

To oven roast:

Set the oven to 350 / 180 degrees

Wash the nuts, drain the water and add salt.

Put the nuts in an oven tray and place in the oven. Keep turning every 5 -10 mins using a wooden spoon for 25 mins or until the nuts are crunchy and have turned slightly brown on the inside. To check the colour, get a few nuts; remove the husks to reveal the nut. Take care not to burn your hands in the hot oven!

Remove from the oven and leave on the side to cool.

Eat as a snack with tea.

On the cooker:

Wash the nuts, add salt and place in a pan and dry roast over medium heat.

Keep turning using a wooden spoon for 25 - 30 mins. To check if the nuts are ready, rub off the skin or husks and if it is slightly brown, then it is ready.

Remove from the fire and leave to cool.

Using a microwave:

Add the washed salted nuts into a microwave oven dish and roast for 5 mins, open the oven and stir, then leave it for another 5 mins.

Variations:

Roast sesame and pumpkin seeds separately and mix with the roasted groundnuts.

Storage:

Keep the roasted groundnuts in a tight sealed container for later use.

Groundnut Sauce – 'Epila / Epilili'

6 tbsp. Smooth groundnut paste

1 medium onion finely chopped

1 large tomato chopped

Curry powder

Salt to taste

Method 1:

1. Add water to a pan, add onions, tomatoes and cook for 10 mins.
2. Add curry powder and salt to taste
3. Stir in the peanut butter, cook for another 5 mins
4. It is ready! Eat with millet bread, *matooke*, rice, *posho*, sweet potatoes or cassava.

Groundnut Curry sauce

Ingredients

2 tbsp. olive oil

6 tbsp. groundnut paste

2 medium sized Onions (finely chopped)

3 large Tomatoes (finely chopped)

½ tsp. mixed spice

½ tsp. Turmeric Powder

½ tsp. Chili Powder

Salt to taste

1. In a large pan, heat olive oil and add onions and cook till the onions turn soft and translucent and add turmeric powder, mixed spice, chilli powder and stir for 1 min. Add tomatoes and salt. Let the tomatoes cook till they are pulpy.
2. Simmer till the gravy reduces slightly and becomes thicker. This will take about 5 mins. At this point, add groundnut paste with some water if you need to adjust the consistency.
3. Delicious with *matooke*, rice or sweet potatoes.

Steamed Groundnut sauce in banana leaves

Although banana plantations were not a main crop in Teso, with migration and movement of people, bananas are now grown in many areas of Teso, and bananas are sold in all markets in Teso.

Ingredients

1 cup of raw groundnuts blended to a powder or paste

1 medium size onion finely chopped

¼ tsp. Black pepper

½ tsp. Curry powder

½ tsp. Cumin powder

5 tender banana leaves

½ tsp salt

½ cup of water

This dish is prepared using banana leaves and it is usually served as a delicacy at functions such as a marriage ceremony or any family gathering.

Method:

1. Mix the groundnut powder with water and add all the seasoning. The mixture should be thick enough to run off a spoon, but not runny and not too thick. Add the finely chopped onion.
2. Singe the tender banana leaves over a fire to make a foil. With a bowl to support the leaves, arrange the leaves inside the dish making sure they overlap to make a dish like shape; place the groundnut paste in the leaves and tie it up using dry banana fibre.
3. The parcel can be dropped into a pan of boiling water or placed on top of a bundle of *matooke* to be steamed for 1 hour.
4. Serve with *matooke*, sweet potatoes or rice.

Note: This method of cooking can be used for other dishes such as chicken, meat, fish and greens.

Variations:

- Add mushrooms to the mixture before placing in the leaves ready for steaming. Absolutely delicious with *matooke*.

Boiled Groundnuts

This method uses freshly picked groundnuts and provides a quick snack during groundnut harvest time. The nuts are boiled in their pods or shells.

1. Pluck the groundnuts off the stems.
2. Wash thoroughly to remove any soil.
3. Add to a pan of water – enough to cover the groundnuts, add salt if required.
4. Boil the nuts for 30 mins.
5. Remove from the fire and put aside to cool.
6. Shell the cooked nuts before eating.

The fresh groundnuts can also be roasted with their shells on an open fire by lighting the dried plants and shrubs over the pods and turning them using a stick until the nuts are cooked. These are shelled and eaten as a snack. Provides a good snack for those harvesting the nuts as groundnuts can be roasted in the garden.

Sesame seeds (*Seasamum indicum*) – 'Ikanyum / Nino'

This crop is grown widely in Teso. Like groundnuts, sesame seeds, also known as 'simsim' can be fried/roasted and eaten as a snack, made into sesame cakes or made into sesame paste to be used to enhance leafy and meat sauces. The sesame paste or butter can be used as a spread on bread and as a side accompaniment for dishes such as cassava or potato dishes. It can also be served on its own as a stew/sauce. Sesame oil is one of the vegetable oils widely used in Teso. Sesame seeds are full of carbohydrate, fats, protein, Vitamin B6 and Minerals (calcium, iron, manganese, sodium and potassium).

Sesame balls

This is a simple snack enjoyed by many, especially children.

Ingredients:

2 ½ cups sesame seeds

½ cup sugar

½ cup honey

1 squeeze lemon juice

Method:

1. Add the cleaned sesame seeds in a wide pan and dry roast for 10 mins. The sesame seeds should turn light brown.
2. In a separate pan, melt the sugar, honey and a squeeze of lemon juice over medium heat and keep stirring for 5 mins.
3. Reduce the heat and add the sesame seeds and stir the mixture together. Remove from the heat.
4. Using a spoon, scoop the mixture and shape into round balls. The mixture may be hot, so take care when handling. Alternatively, spread the hot mixture over a moulded tray.
5. The balls can be flattened to make small round cakes.
6. To make bars, roll out the mixture on to a greased baking paper. Place another baking sheet over it. Using a rolling pin, roll out the mixture to a required thickness.
7. Leave to set for 10 mins.
8. Remove the paper and cut into the required shape.

Bambara Nuts (*Vigna subterranean*) – 'Isuk'

Bambara nuts are legume plants grown mainly for subsistence use. Bambara nuts grow like the groundnut in that the pods grow and ripen underground and come in many varieties, red, white and black.

Bambara nuts are rich in calcium. The nuts can be eaten fresh by boiling, or roasting them in their pods. The dried nuts can be roasted and eaten as a snack. They can also be boiled and mixed with cooked sweet potatoes to give a delicious mash known as *'emangor.'*

When using dried Bambara nuts, soak them in water overnight before cooking or roasting them as a snack.

Fish – 'Agaria'

Fish forms a big part of the diet for most communities living along the lake shores of Kyoga and Bisina in Teso region. Fish provides a good source of high protein and Vitamins (A, D, E and K) and minerals. Fish is also healthy because of its low-fat value and because of its oily nature. It is rich in Omega 3 fatty acids, the good fats.

The nutrients and minerals in fish, and particularly the Omega-3 fatty acids found in oily fish are good for the heart and can make improvements in brain development and reproduction.

Smoked fish and dried fish in groundnut sauce is widely consumed in Teso and is considered a delicacy. Fish can also be eaten fresh using a variety of cooking methods such as steaming, roasting, boiling and frying.

There are 4 particular types of fish found in the waters of Teso:

1. Catfish – 'Ebileng / Rec'
2. Tilapia – 'Aporogit / Aporogo'
3. Silver fish – 'Aiyoi'
4. Snake like slippery fish – 'Ekole'

Smoked Fish in groundnut sauce – Traditional version

You can use any type of smoked or dried fish but in this recipe, I am using the catfish – ' *Ebileng'*

The fish is gutted, descaled and washed. It is dried over coal fire and sometimes dried in the sun.

Ingredients:

1 whole large smoked fish cut into medium pieces

2 tbsp. liquid soda ash (*abalang*)

Salt to taste

Dried mushrooms (optional).

Method:

1. Wash the fish and leave to soak in water. Remove the bones where possible.
2. Sort and clean the dried mushrooms, and soak in water.
3. In a large pan, bring water to boil, add the fish, salt to taste and cover. Halfway through the cooking add the mushrooms, add the liquid soda ash and leave to simmer.
4. Mix the ground nut paste in warm water to the required consistency and pour over the fish, stir and cover to simmer.
5. Delicious with millet bread.

Smoked Fish in groundnut stew – Modern version

You can use any type of smoked or dried fish but in this recipe, I am using the tilapia – 'Aporogit'

Ingredients

1 whole large smoked fish cut into small pieces – remove any bones

2 tbsp. olive oil

4 tbsp. ground nut paste

2 medium sized onions (finely chopped)

3 large Tomatoes (finely chopped)

1/2 tsp Turmeric Powder

1/2 tsp Chili Powder

Salt to taste

Method

1. Wash the fish and leave it to soak in water

Make the ground nut sauce

1. In a large pan, heat olive oil and add onions and cook till the onions turn soft and translucent. Then add tomatoes, turmeric powder and salt.
2. Stir and bring this to a boil. Simmer and let the tomatoes cook till they are pulpy. This will take about 5mins. At this point, add groundnut paste with some water if you need to adjust the consistency.
3. Add the fish, season and cover. Leave to simmer for 10 mins or until cooked.
4. Serve hot with millet bread, *matooke* or sweet potatoes.

Fresh Steamed Fish

The dish is usually made with a whole fish including the head. In this recipe, I am using Tilapia.

Ingredients

1 medium Tilapia fish (gutted, cleaned and washed)

3 tbsp. Vegetable oil

2 tbsp. lemon juice

2 medium onions (peeled and chopped)

3 medium tomatoes (chopped)

1 clove of garlic (peeled and crushed)

Salt and black pepper

Method:

1. In a large pan, heat up the oil, add onions and fry until golden brown.
2. Add garlic, tomatoes, salt and black pepper, and mix well.
3. Season the fish with lemon juice, salt and black pepper and place the fish in the pan. Spoon the sauce over it, and cover and simmer for 15 minutes or until the fish is cooked.
4. Serve hot with greens and any staple food.

Steamed fish in banana leaves

Ingredients:

1 medium Tilapia fish

1 small onion

2 cloves of garlic (crushed)

1 tsp coarse black pepper

¼ tsp salt

5 tender banana leaves and a string of dry banana fibre

Method:

1. Clean and season the fish using salt, black pepper, onions and garlic.
2. Singe the tender banana leaves over a fire to make a foil. Place the fish in the leaves and tie it up using dry banana fibre.
3. The parcel can be dropped into a pan of boiling water or placed on top of a bundle of matooke to be steamed.

Delicious with *matooke*

Silver fish (*Rastrineobola argentea*) – 'Aiyoi / Onang'

Silver fish is found in the waters of most lakes in Uganda.

Silver fish has got nutrients such as vitamin A and E and fatty oils that prevent poor vision and promote good skin texture. Silver fish is also said to contain good iron levels. It also acts as animal feed, with poultry farmers adding silver fish as a nutrient to their chicken feeds. (5)

Ingredients:

A cupful of silver fish (250 grams)

2 Ripe tomatoes

1 tbsp. Cooking oil

1 medium onion

1 bunch of Coriander

1 clove of garlic (optional)

1 Green chilli (optional)

Water

Salt to taste

1 Royco cube/Maggi cube

½ sliced lemon

Method:

1. Remove dirt from the silver fish, and wash in lukewarm water.
2. Add the silver fish to a pot of water and boil for a minimum 30 minutes.
3. Cut onions into small pieces then fry until golden brown.
4. Add Garlic and fry slightly.
5. Add Tomatoes followed by coriander.
6. Drain all the water from boiled silver fish then add to the tomato sauce; cook for 2 minutes.
7. Add Royco/Maggi cube and salt to taste then stir.
8. Add water, boil for 3-5 minutes.
9. Serve then squeeze some lemon on the silver fish while on the table.
10. Best served with hot *posho* and vegetables (e.g. spinach, greens).

Variations:

- Silver fish can also be added to other sauces such as meat or spinach greens.
- Silver fish can be made into powder which can be added to other dishes especially for children.

Fried Fish

Ingredients:

2 large Tilapia fish

1 tbsp. butter, melted.

1 tsp fish seasoning.

½ tsp dried parsley flakes.

¼ tsp paprika.

¼ tsp dried thyme.

Oil

For the side sauce:

1 medium onion (chopped)

3 green chillies (chopped)

1 large tomato (chopped)

Method:

1. Heat oil in a deep-fryer or large saucepan to 350 degrees F (180 degrees C).
2. Rinse the fish and dry well.
3. Make shallow slits or cuts on the fish, Mix the seasoning and rub into the fish.
4. Gently slip the fish into the oil and fry until crispy, for 7 to 10 minutes.
5. While the fish drains, heat 2 tablespoons oil in a large pan.
6. Cook and stir the chili peppers, garlic, and onion in the hot oil until lightly browned, 5 to 7 minutes. Add the chopped tomatoes into the mixture and remove from heat.
7. Spoon the sauce over the fish and serve hot. The sauce can be placed on the side.
8. Serve with *matooke*, salad and a fresh lemon

Meat – *Akiring*

Apart from subsistence farming, the Iteso also practice traditional livestock keeping practices such as rearing of cattle, goats, sheep, chicken which continue to provide food and livelihood alternatives for most households. Cows remain central to the post nomadic lifestyle, providing milk, beef, ghee, skin, dung –all of which were used outdoors then, and in the home today. Cattle are also used for marriage as bride price.

Smoked meat in groundnut sauce – Traditional Version

You can use meat that has already been smoked and dried or freshly smoked beef. In this recipe, I am using the dried meat. For best results, use a clay pot for cooking.

Ingredients:

1 kg meat on the bone – already smoked and dried

300g ground nuts paste

50g Mushrooms

50g muskmelon – preferably already cooked - optional

3 tbsp. Liquid soda ash

½ tsp Salt

Method:

1. Soak the meat in cold water for 1 hour
2. Add water to the pot and bring to boil.
3. Wash the meat and add to the pot; the water should just cover the meat, leave to cook on low heat for 30 mins. Leave for longer if the meat is tough.
4. Add liquid soda ash, mushrooms and salt to taste. Leave to cook for another 20 minutes.
5. If using already cooked muskmelon, add to the mix.
6. In a separate dish, mix the groundnut paste into a smooth thick consistency using water and some of the soup from the pot.
7. Add to the pot and mix to the desired consistency. If too thick, add hot water and if runny, add more groundnut paste.
8. Delicious with millet bread or any of the staple foods.

Smoked meat in groundnut sauce – Modern Version

Ingredients:

1 kg meat on the bone

300gms ground nuts paste

1 large onion

1 large tomato

1 green pepper

1 tsp oil

1 tsp curry powder

½ tsp of ginger powder

½ tsp ground black pepper

1½ litres hot water

Salt to taste

Method:

1. Smoke the large chunks of meat in coal until brown and almost cooked.
2. Cut the smoked meat into medium sized pieces.
3. Chop the onions, tomatoes and peppers into small pieces.
4. Heat the oil in the pan and add onions. Stir until the onions turn golden brown.
5. Add curry powder, ginger and black pepper; cook for 2 mins.
6. Add tomatoes and cook until soft.
7. Add the hot water, meat and peppers and bring to boil.
8. Cover the pan and let it cook for 20 minutes.
9. Mix the groundnut paste into a smooth paste and add to the boiling meat. Keep stirring for a smooth consistency. Add more water if required.
10. Cover and reduce the heat to a simmer and cook for another 10 minutes.
11. Serve hot with any of the following staple foods: millet bread, posho, matooke, rice.

- Roast the meat in the oven until almost cooked to get the same results as using coal except you don't get the smoky flavour you get from an open fire.

Boiled meat.

A very simple method of cooking meat without hassle. Use a clay pot or a slow cooker for best results.

500g meat

2 onions

2 large tomatoes

1 tsp salt

1 tsp curry powder

½ cabbage

Method:

1. Wash the meat and put in a pot or saucepan with a lid, add water and bring to boil.
2. After 30 mins, chop and add onions, tomatoes, cabbage and curry powder and salt. Reduce heat and leave to cook slowly until meat is soft and tender.
3. Nice to eat on its own as soup or eat with any staple dish.

Beef Stew.

Ingredients:

500g meat

2 onions (chopped)

2 large tomatoes

1 tbsp. tomato puree

3 teaspoonful cooking oil

1 tbsp. crushed garlic

1 tbsp. crushed ginger

1 tsp salt

1 tsp curry powder

1tsp mixed spice

1 tsp paprika

2 stock or Maggi cubes

2 carrots chopped to medium pieces

1. Cut meat (beef) into small pieces and wash. Drain all the water.
2. Using half the garlic, ginger paste and 1 Maggi cube, add to the meat, mix and set aside for 20 mins to marinade.
3. Heat the oil in a large pan, add onions and fry for 2 mins, add the rest of the garlic and ginger and fry till the onions are golden brown, add the rest of the seasoning and fry for 2 mins.
4. Add the meat with all its juices to the pan, mix and cover with a well-fitting lid.
5. Cook the meat in its juices for 30 mins, stirring occasionally.
6. Add fresh chopped or blended tomatoes, puree and the remaining cube and cook for 15 mins.
7. If required, add water to cover half the meat, and let it cook until the meat is tender.
8. Serve with rice, millet bread or mashed green bananas.

Roast Meat.

Roasting meat is done over a smoky coal fire. The meat is seasoned, put in skewers and roasted over the fire, turning occasionally and sprinkling it with water to make sure it does not burn. The meat can be served with salad, roast plantain, cassava or it can be eaten on its own. In Teso, meats like chicken and fish are roasted over open fire and eaten on any occasion.

Cow Foot – 'Emolokony'

Most people cringe at the thought of eating the foot of any animal, but in many African cultures, especially in Teso, this part of the animal is cooked as a delicacy commonly known as 'emolokony'. This dish can be eaten with the broth as a soup or simply eaten as is. Bone broth contains a high quantity of the vital minerals calcium and phosphorus, and is high in collagen and elastin which is beneficial for supporting strong bones.

Some doctors will recommend people with arthritis to eat cow foot soup

The best way to cook cow foot is by using a clay pot or a slow cooker. For 'emolokony' to be fully appreciated, it must be cooked until it is very tender and falling off the bones. It is usual to find other parts of the animal such as the head also prepared and added to 'emolokony' to be cooked together.

Tip: You can get away with using just onions, salt and pepper and still end up with a delicious dish of 'emolokony'.

Ingredients:

2 lbs Cow Foot

2 cloves of garlic (crushed)

2 sprig of thyme

2 stock cubes

2 onions chopped

1 whole scotch bonnet pepper (optional)

Salt and black pepper

1. Place the cow's foot, onion, garlic, salt, pepper and water into a large saucepan. Bring the water to a boil over high heat.
2. Add the whole scotch bonnet, stock cubes. Reduce the heat to medium-low and simmer the cow's foot until it is soft and tender, and falling off the bone.
3. Serve it hot and eat on its own or with millet bread or *matooke*.

Oxtail

Oxtail is prepared and enjoyed the same way as cow foot. It is best slow cooked in a pot until it is soft and tender and falling off the bone. It can be eaten as broth or soup and can be eaten with millet bread, rice or green bananas.

Abdominal Offal – 'Amoeteka'

Offal, also commonly referred to as 'organ meats' also includes the heart, liver, lungs, kidneys, pancreas and all other abdominal organs, as well as the tails, feet, brain, tongue, tripe, and yes, even the testicles. (6)

What are the benefits of Offal?

They contain a wide spectrum of nutrients like B-complex vitamins, vitamins E, D and K2, amino acids, iron, and trace minerals like copper, chromium, and zinc.

The recipe below is for abdominal offal i.e. intestines and the stomach (towels), commonly known in Ateso as 'amoeteka keda aboin'.

After the animal is slaughtered, it is common to prepare the 'offal' as a separate dish.

> 250g offal
>
> 1 clove of garlic
>
> 2 large onions
>
> 2 beef cubes
>
> 4 large ripe, red tomatoes blanched
>
> 1 tbsp. Royco
>
> 1 level tbsp. tomato paste
>
> 2 tbsp ghee
>
> 3 medium-size carrots
>
> Salt

Method:

To blanch the tomatoes, add them to a pot of boiling water and leave for 2 mins.
Remove from the hot water, peel off and discard the skin and chop roughly.

1. Cut the offal into bite-size pieces and wash thoroughly, in several washes of water.
2. Put offal in a sauce pan and just cover with salted water. Cover the pan, bring to the boil, reduce the heat and simmer covered until cooked.
3. Meanwhile, chop onions, crush garlic and slice carrots to a medium-size thickness.
4. Heat the ghee and fry the onions adding in the garlic and carrots when the onions begin to brown.
5. Mix the tomatoes with the tomato paste, crumbled up beef cubes and a little salt and add to the onion mixture. Reduce the heat, cover pan and simmer until tomatoes are cooked.
6. Add in the offal. Swirl warm water in the pan the offal were cooked in and pour it in as well making sure there is enough water to cover the offal. Cover and simmer for another 10 mins.
7. Delicious with millet bread or green bananas.

Chicken – 'Akokor'

Eggs

Eggs are rarely eaten as they are left to be hatched into chicks. However when eaten they are normally eaten as boiled eggs. Eggs can also be prepared as a sauce in peanut butter and eaten with any staple food.

Egg in groundnut Sauce

Preparation Time: 30 minutes

Ingredients:

5 hard-boiled eggs (peeled)

2 tbsp. olive oil

4 tbsp. peanut butter

2 medium sized Onions (finely chopped)

3 large Tomatoes (finely chopped)

½ tsp. Turmeric Powder

½ tsp. Chili Powder

Salt to taste

Method:

1. In a large pan, heat olive oil and add the onions and fry till they are golden brown.
2. Add turmeric and chilli powder, stir and add tomatoes and salt. Let it cook for 5 mins.
3. Mix the groundnut paste with water and add to the pan.
4. Cut the eggs in half (or use whole) and drop the eggs in the sauce, cover and let it stand for five minutes before serving.

Variation:

- Instead of boiled eggs, the raw eggs can be broken and scrambled directly on to the peanut sauce and cooked till they are firm, like scrambled eggs. Delicious with rice.

Boiled Chicken

Chicken is reared in most homesteads as domestic fowl and is normally a source of income for families. On rare occasions, during celebrations or when visitors are hosted, chicken forms part of the main food item. It is common to find chicken roasted along the road side to provide on the go snacks for travellers.

I remember the routine very clearly. When the visitor arrived, my mother would identify a chicken among so many roaming around. We would be asked to 'catch' the chicken for slaughter. We would chase the chicken sometimes for 20 minutes or more especially if you found a clever chicken. It would fly up the tree, down the bushes back into the compound, even run into the house (where the visitors were seated) and out again. By the time you caught the poor thing, you were all so exhausted the only thing in your minds was 'wait till you get on the plate'. There was always one person tasked with slaughtering the chicken. We all knew the routine of de feathering and then slicing the chicken to the agreed sections.

The recipe below is for free range chicken which is slightly tougher than the reared ones.

Ingredients

1 large chicken, cut into pieces

1 large onion (diced)

2 large tomatoes (chopped)

1 tsp curry powder

Salt to taste

Method:

1. Add water to a large pan or pot and bring to boil.
2. Wash the chicken and add to the boiling water. Cover the pan or pot and leave chicken to cook.
3. After 30 mins, stir in the onions, tomatoes and salt and curry powder.
4. Reduce the fire and leave to cook slowly until chicken is tender.
5. Serve with mashed green bananas, millet bread, rice or *posho*.

Smoked Chicken in groundnut sauce

Ingredients:

1 large chicken, cut into pieces

1 large onion (diced)

2 large tomatoes (chopped)

1 tsp curry powder

6 tbsp. groundnut paste

Salt to taste

Method:

1. Smoke the chicken over hot coal turning regularly until half cooked.
2. Place the smoked chicken into a pot of boiling water, just enough water to cover the chicken, add the onions, tomatoes, curry powder and salt. Stir and cover; reduce the heat and leave the chicken to simmer until it is ready.
3. Mix the peanut butter using the soup from the pot of cooking chicken and pour the mixture into the pot. Add water if required.
4. Bring to boil and remove from heat.
5. Delicious with millet bread or sweet potatoes or *posho*.

BBQ Style Roast Chicken legs

This is a very quick, easy and delicious recipe for the busy, no time person. The amount of chicken you use depends on the numbers you are cooking for. However, for this recipe I am using 6 chicken legs. The result is tender chicken that comes off the bone easily with a barbecue-style charred appearance and flavour. It's so easy anyone can do it; just put it in the oven and leave it to do its magic.

This is what I call a modern recipe as using an oven for cooking was rare. Instead, the chicken legs would be placed on a rack and roasted over hot coals of fire giving you the same charred appearance but this time with a smoky flavour.

Ingredients:

6 chicken legs with skin on

For marinade

2 tbsp tomato puree

6 tbsp tomato ketchup

3 tbsp. Worcester sauce *or* BBQ sauce

2 tbsp. chicken seasoning

2 tbsp runny honey

1 clove of garlic (crushed)

Method:

1. Use a sharp knife to make shallow slits in the top of the chicken legs.
2. Place all the ingredients for the marinade in a large bowl and stir until mixed. Add the chicken legs and toss to coat, using your hands to cover them really well in the marinade. Cover the bowl and put aside in a cool place to marinate for a minimum of 30 minutes.
3. Meanwhile, preheat the oven to 180°C/200°C and line a roasting tin with foil.
4. Place the marinated chicken legs in the lined tin, skin side up in a single layer, and spoon over the remaining marinade from the bowl. Roast in the oven for 35–40 minutes until sticky and golden and cooked through. Skim off any fat from the cooking juices and pour the juices into a jug.
5. Serve hot with the juices poured over, and with a green vegetable and baby potatoes or mash on the side.

Finger Millet (*Eleusine coracana*) – 'Alos / Kal'

Finger Millet is a very important part of the local diet in Teso and is an excellent source of natural calcium which helps in strengthening bones for growing children and aging people. Regular consumption of finger millet is good for bone health and keeps diseases such as osteoporosis at bay and could reduce the risk of fractures. Finger millet is also a very good source of iron and is known to help in the recovery from anaemia. Because millet is high in fibre, it is also recommended for other conditions such as diabetes, high blood pressure and it is known to boost the immune system; to name a few. (7)

Millet is also the main ingredient used in the making of a popular brew in Teso known as '*Ajon*'

Millet Bread – 'Atap'

Millet bread is the main staple food eaten in Teso. The bread is made out of a mixture of millet and cassava flour. It can also be made from a mixture of sorghum and cassava flour, dried sweet potatoes and cassava flour, commonly known as 'aduda' or cassava and maize flour and it can also be made from just millet flour or cassava flour.

To make millet bread 'atap'

Ingredients:

> Millet flour
>
> Tamarind extract or any other flavouring agent
>
> Water

Mix millet with cassava and sorghum (optional) and grind into flour. Ratio of millet to cassava varies and also depends on availability.

Tamarind water is extracted from the tamarind soaked in water and used to flavour the millet bread.

Other ingredients used to flavour the millet bread are lemon juice, water extracted from boiled unripe small mangoes.

Method:

1. Soak the tamarind in cold water and extract the juice. Lemon juice may be used as a substitute for tamarind.
2. Add to a pan, add water and bring to boil
3. Gradually add the flour to the boiling water while mixing quickly using a wooden stick to make sure lumps of flour don't form.
4. Keep adding the flour until you get a stiff sticky dough.
5. Serve hot with any of the Teso pasted dishes.

Millet porridge – *"Akima"*

Cooking Time: 20 mins

Serves: 2

4 heaped tbsp. millet flour

2 cup tamarind liquid

1 cup warm water

3 tbsp. sugar

Method:

1. Mix the warm water with the flour to a smooth consistency. This is to avoid lumps forming during cooking.
2. Add the tamarind liquid and place the pan on a low heat; stir continuously.
3. Keep stirring until the porridge is cooked.
4. Add sugar to taste.
5. Serve hot.

Variations:

- Sour milk can be added to the porridge during cooking. Millet porridge is said to be very nutritious especially for breast feeding mums as it is said to enhance the milk production and its iron rich properties.
- Mix millet flour with soya flour to make porridge especially for young children.

Sorghum (*Sorghum bicolor*) – '*Imumwa / Bel*'

Sorghum is a cereal grain crop which grows well in many different environments; it is naturally drought tolerant and is versatile as a food, feed and fuel. In Teso, sorghum is mixed with dried cassava and ground into flour to make sorghum bread which accompanies most dishes. Sorghum can also be made into porridge. Sorghum is high in carbohydrates, protein and fat and contains calcium and small amounts of iron, vitamin B1 and niacin.

Sorghum, like millet, is an important source of income for women who process it into various fermented and non-fermented beverages.

Because sorghum is drought resistant some areas in Teso have started growing it for livestock feed.

Cassava (*Manihot esculenta*) – '*Emuogo*'

Cassava is a tropical root vegetable grown and consumed in most parts of Teso. Cassava is high in carbohydrates and provides fibre, vitamins and some minerals though in small quantities. As flour, it has many food uses and is one of the best alternatives to wheat and other grains, even for celiac patients. Some of the benefits of cassava are that it contains resistant starch which is beneficial because it feeds the friendly bacteria in your colon which turn it into important short-chain fatty acids. It feeds good gut bacteria and may lower your blood glucose levels. (8)

Cassava can be eaten in various forms, boiled and eaten as a snack, roasted, fried into chips. It can also be dried and preserved for later use during the dry season.

Cassava in its dried form is mixed with millet, sorghum or dried sweet potatoes and ground into flour from which '*Atap*' (millet bread) is produced.

Cassava is also a source of income for most households in all its states .i.e. raw, dried, flour, cassava stems and it can also be processed into a very potent gin called '*eguli*' or '*waragi*'.

Boiled Cassava

Preparation Time: 5 mins

Cooking Time: 15 mins

Serves: 4

Ingredients:

1. 2 medium size cassava roots peeled and cubed
2. Salt to season (optional)
3. Butter for flavour (optional)

Method:

1. Place the chunks of peeled cassava root in the boiling water, or a steamer and allow them to cook until the root is very soft when poked with a fork.
2. Place on a plate and add butter or seasoning if required

Boiled cassava can be served with tea, eaten as a snack or can be used to accompany any of the dishes such as peanut sauce; peanut butter as a dip. It can also be served with any cooked greens on the side eg spinach, kale.

Boiled mashed Cassava

Peel the cassava, wash and cut into small pieces. Place in a pan of water and boil until soft.

Mash the cassava and serve with any sauce; but it is delicious with groundnut sauce!.

Cassava Chips

Ingredients:

1. 4 large cassava peeled and chopped into large chunks.
2. Oil for frying.
3. Sea salt to flavour.

Preparation Time: 15 mins

Cooking Time: 45 minutes

Serves: 4

Method:

1. Bring a large pan of salted water to boil and add the cassava chunks. Boil until tender, around 30 minutes, then drain and allow to cool slightly.
2. Heat the oil in a large, heavy based saucepan until smoking hot, and then, working in batches, add the cassava and deep fry until golden brown.
3. Lay each batch on kitchen paper to soak up excess oil, then sprinkle liberally with sea salt. Serve piping hot with grilled meat or chicken and lots of spicy hot sauce.

Cassava pancakes – 'Ecokil'

It is a pancake made from cassava flour mixed with sweet ripe bananas. The mixture is formed into little pancakes and deep fried. They are crispy on the outside and soft and gooey on the inside. Super delicious!

Ingredients:

4 cups of cassava flour

½ cup of plain flour

½ cup of corn meal flour

3 very ripe bananas

3 tbsp. sugar or more for sweeter taste

¼ tsp cinnamon to flavour

½ tsp ginger powder

Oil

Method:

1. Add the different types of flour, banana and sugar into a bowl.
2. Mix together into a firm mixture. Add cinnamon and ginger powder.
3. Shape into round balls and flatten to form small pancakes.
4. Deep fry in hot oil until they are golden brown.
5. Remove and put on a kitchen paper to soak up any oil.
6. Delicious with a cup of tea.

Yams (*Dioscorea alata*) – "Abatot"

Yams are tuber crops that are grown in some areas in Teso. Yams are usually found growing in swampy areas and they are available almost throughout the year. Yams are said to be rich in Vitamin 6 and are full of potassium. Yams are prepared and eaten as a snack or as a main meal usually with beans. To prepare yams, wash them thoroughly to remove the soil and boil with or without their skin. Yams can also be steamed or roasted.

Sweet Potatoes (*Ipomoea batatas*) – 'Acok / Kata'

Sweet potatoes are a root vegetable grown in most parts of Teso. They are a rich source of fibre as well as containing a good array of vitamins and minerals including iron, calcium, selenium, and they're a good source of most of our B vitamins and vitamin C.

Like cassava, sweet potatoes can be eaten in various forms, boiled, roasted, dried, turned into flour and used to accompany other foods or mixed with other foods to form delicacies that are enjoyed throughout the region. In its dried form, sweet potatoes are preserved as *'amukeke'* one of the delicacies from Teso region.

Boiled Sweet Potatoes

Preparation Time: 5 mins

Cooking Time: 15 mins

Serves: 4

Ingredients:

4 medium sized Sweet Potatoes peeled and cut into pieces

Method:

1. Place the potatoes into a pan of boiling water. Cook until soft to touch.
2. Sweet potatoes can also be steamed using banana leaves.

Clay baked potatoes – 'Emukaro'

The most popular sweet potato dish is called 'Emukaro'- potatoes baked in clay.

Serves: 6

1. Wash 6 medium sized potatoes and put aside.
2. Dig a hole in the ground.
3. Lumps of soil or bricks
4. Using bricks or lumps of soil make an 'igloo' shaped oven by carefully arranging the bricks to form a semi-circle. Leave room or an opening so you can place the potatoes.
5. Light a fire and bake the bricks or the clay. Once the soil is red hot, remove the ash from the hole.
6. Place the potatoes inside the hole. Potatoes can be wrapped in banana leaves or foil if available before placing them in the hole.
7. Collapse the hot clay / bricks onto the potatoes and cover the mound with soil
8. Leave overnight or for 5 to six hours
9. Remove the clay to get the baked potatoes.
10. Delicious in the morning with tea.

Dried sliced potatoes – 'Amukeke'

To make *amukeke*, potatoes are peeled and sliced into thin slices.

These are sun dried to make *amukeke*.

Amukeke Dish.

1. Soak the dried *amukeke* in cold water for 1 hour.
2. Add to a pan of boiling water. The water should just cover the *amukeke*.
3. Cover and let it cook for 1 hour or until soft. It will turn brown and soft.
4. Using a stick, mingle / mash the *amukeke* into a soft mash. Add the peanut butter and ghee mixture and mingle together.
5. Delicious with groundnut sauce

Cooked amukeke is also delicious as a snack served with a cup of tea

Variation:

- Dried amukeke can be mixed with cassava and ground into flour to make millet bread

Sweet Potato chips – Oven baked

Ingredients:

4 medium sized sweet potatoes peeled and sliced lengthwise into medium pieces

2 tbsp. olive oil

1 tbsp. mixed herbs

¼ **tsp** salt

Method:

1. Heat the oven to 350 F (180C)
2. Mix together the potatoes, olive oil, herbs and salt
3. Place the potatoes in an oven tray
4. Place in the oven and bake/roast for 45 mins or until the potatoes are slightly brown
5. Serve as a snack with tea or as a side dish

Maize – 'Ekirididi'

Maize is widely grown throughout Teso region. When ripe or mature, the maize can be eaten in various forms. It can be boiled or roasted and eaten usually off the cob. In its ground form, maize is the main food served in schools, hospitals and in households as porridge and maize meal 'posho'. Maize husks are also used as feed and fodder for livestock and poultry and the dried stems can be used to thatch houses and to feed animals as well.

Grilled/Roasted Maize

Roasted maize is one of the most popular on-the-go snacks eaten throughout Teso. Mature corn (maize) is picked and roasted over hot coal and when cool, is eaten off the cob.

Boiled Maize

Mature corn (maize) is picked and placed in a pan with its covers. The maize is boiled for 30 mins or until it is ready. Remove the covers before eating.

Maize meal (Posho) – "Euga"

Posho is a common food made from maize meal and is consumed throughout Teso.

The cornmeal (maize meal) is added to boiling water and mingled until it turns into a dense cornmeal paste.

Maize meal is widely used in Teso especially in schools and hospitals. Porridge made out of maize meal provides a quick morning snack for most families before the start of a days work.

Posho can be eaten with any leafy dishes, meat stews. It can also be used as a side dish served with roast meat or chicken.

Green Bananas / Plantain – 'Etaget'

Green bananas commonly known as *'matooke'* are not native to Teso. However, migration, intermarriage and general change in farming choices has meant that green banana plantations are now found all over Teso. Green bananas are also sold in markets throughout Teso. It is therefore not unusual to find green bananas served as a main dish in some households in Teso.

Green bananas are said to be rich in potassium which is a key ingredient in regulating blood pressure.

To prepare a green banana meal or 'matooke', as it is commonly known:

1. Peel and wash the green bananas
2. Add water to a pan, and arrange banana leaves in the pan making sure they overlap.
3. Place the *'matooke'* on the leaves and cover the *'matooke'* with the overlapping leaves. Using more banana leaves, cover the *'matooke'* completely.
4. Steam the *'matooke'* until it is ready.
5. Mash the *'matooke'*, cover with the leaves used for cooking, and leave it on low heat to simmer. The leaves give the bananas a very good smoky flavour
6. Best served with groundnut sauce, beef, chicken or beans.

Variations:

- Boil or steam the bananas, add salt, onions, tomatoes and peanut butter to give you a delicious morning or midday snack.
- Cook the offal until they are ready. Peel and add the green bananas and continue cooking on low heat until they are ready. Delicious!
- Fry onions till golden brown, add seasoning, tomatoes and green peppers. Add salt and water. Add the peeled bananas and cook on medium heat till they are soft and tender.

Rice – 'Emuceri'

Rice is grown in many parts of Teso mainly as a cash crop but it is also consumed in many households. Rice is the main food served during celebrations and it is also served in schools and hospitals.

The most common method of cooking rice is boiling. However, during special occasions, it is common to find 'pilau' rice being prepared.

There are many recipes of 'pilau' rice but I have chosen to use one by my nieces.

Pilau **Rice**[6]

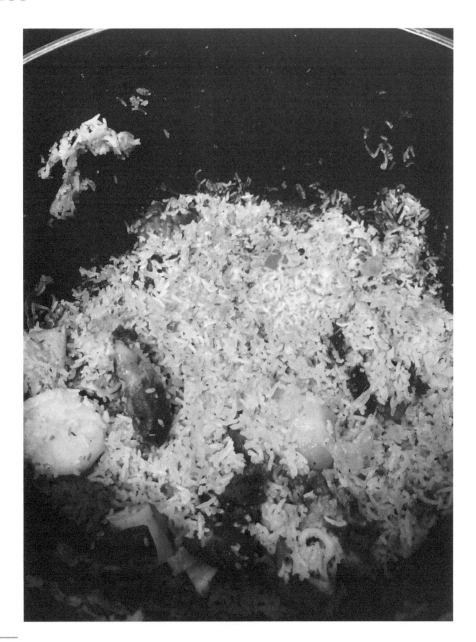

6 Recipe of pilau, mandazi and chapatti by my nieces Sabah and Sabra

Ingredients:

1kg of meat or ½ kg if you prefer less meat

4 measuring cups of rice, wash and soak it for 1/2 hour

2 to 3 medium to large size onions

1 tbsp. crushed garlic

1 tbsp. crushed ginger

10 to 15 cloves

1 tsp black pepper

1 tsp cardamom

2 medium sticks of cinnamon

2 tbsp. cumin seeds

6 cups of water

Salt to taste

Steps:

1. Boil the meat, add salt and cook till tender.
2. Using a separate saucepan, pour in the oil, add onions, and fry till light brown. If you prefer brown pilau then fry the onions until golden/dark brown.
3. Add in the garlic, ginger and the rest of the seasoning. Fry for roughly 1 minute, then add the meat without its soup. Fry for another minute.
4. Drain the water from the rice and add to the meat. Fry for a roughly 1 minute.
5. Using the soup from the meat as top up to the six cups of water, add to the rice. Note: add salt to your taste.
6. Cook the rice until the water is reduced then turn the heat to very low and let it cook slowly; if you have an oven it is even better once the water is reduced put the 'pilau' in the oven at 220 degrees C for about 45 minutes to 1 hour

After 30 minutes check the rice mix then put it back for about 20 to 25 minutes for the rice to cook soft yet dry.

Optional: You can add in peas, carrots and potatoes to make mixed veg/pilau.

Doughnuts – 'Mandazi'

The recipes for 'mandazi' vary widely; I have used one given to me by my nieces.

Ingredients:

1kg all-purpose plain flour

1 tbsp. instant yeast

8 tbsp. sugar

4 tbsp. oil

250ml lukewarm milk

250ml lukewarm water

Method:

1. Pour the flour in a bowl, add the yeast, sugar, oil and mix well.
2. Add the milk and water slowly as you knead until you get a smooth dough.
3. Using your hand, make medium-sized round roll balls and let the balls rise to double the size, about 30 mins.
4. Roll flat each ball and cut to make 4 triangles
5. Deep fry in medium heat and keep turning until golden brown.

Chapati

There are different ways of making chapatti. The method used here is one used by my nieces.

Ingredients

1kg plain flour

125ml oil

250ml lukewarm water

250ml lukewarm milk (if not an option, add 250ml lukewarm water)

10ml oil (to knead)

10ml lukewarm water (to knead)

1 cup of oil mixed with 1tbsp. ghee (for the frying stage)

Method:

1. Pour the flour in a bowl, add salt and slowly add oil, milk and water. Alternatively, you can mix all the liquids together before using.
2. Knead until you get a soft dough. Add 10ml oil and 10ml water and continue to knead until you get nice smooth dough and it doesn't stick to your hands or the mixing bowl.
3. Using your hand, make medium-sized round roll balls, cover with a tea cloth and leave for 30mins.
4. Heat the flat pan for frying the *chapati*.
5. Roll out one ball at a time and place in the dry, hot pan.
6. Fry in medium heat and then flip the *chapati* over to reveal the cooked side.
7. Using a spoon, add oil to the cooked side. Using a plain piece of paper, press the *chapati* while rotating it to remove the bubbles that may form. (Tip: use the empty flour packaging as the paper.)
8. Turn it over, cook the other side for a few more seconds to give you a golden, cooked *chapati*.
9. Repeat for the rest of the *chapati*.
10. Delicious with meat or chicken stew.

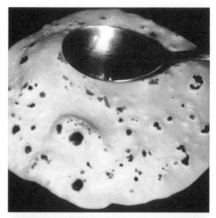

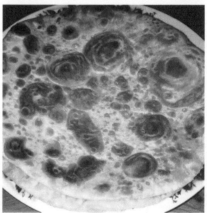

Variation:

- *Chapati* can be eaten as a snack with tea.
- It is also delicious with honey, or cheese spread.

Millet Brew – 'Ajon'

For centuries, the Iteso (people from Teso) have been drinking 'Ajon', a local brew made from dry finger millet. You cannot claim to have been to Teso if you didn't encounter the beautiful food and the drink known as 'Ajon'. From the process involved, I would be right to claim that the Iteso were scientists long before the arrival of foreigners on African soil. 'Ajon' is at the centre of every celebration, a source of income for some families and is also used in exchange for labour; a way of appreciation for the work done. It is also consumed as a beverage and it is usual to find people seated around a pot of 'Ajon' or just passing around a calabash of 'Ajon' in the evening, relaxing after a day's work and generally having a great time. I would not do Teso justice if I didn't include the recipe for the one great drink that has been enjoyed through generations and is now loved by many other people from different parts of Uganda and the world at large. And it is the only alcoholic drink I know that is drunk with hot water.

To make the ingredients for the millet brew, you need finger millet.

1. Thresh and clean the millet to remove the chaff, stones and sand.
2. Grind the millet using a grinding stone. Today, the millet can be ground using a grinding mill.
3. Mix the flour with water to form a thick consistency.
4. Dig a large hole, layer it with banana leaves and put the flour mixture inside the hole. Cover properly using the banana leaves and add soil on top of the leaves to make sure it is sealed properly. (Alternatively,

you can place the mixture in a basket or container that can be sealed.)

5. After seven (7) days, remove the soil and the leaves to get the fermented mixture.
6. Roast over a hot fire using a large roasting pan.
7. Spread the roasted stuff out in the sun to dry.

To make the yeast:

1. While the millet is fermenting, prepare the yeast.
2. Using cleaned millet, put in a container, and generously sprinkle water over the millet.
3. On the second day, mix and add more water, and either leave the millet in the container or pour it out onto a clean floor. Cover the millet using banana leaves if you have them, otherwise use a cloth or sack to cover the millet. The millet will start sprouting or germinating.
4. On the third day, check the millet and mix it again to make sure it is germinating evenly.
5. On the fourth day, spread out the germinated millet under the sun to dry.
6. When dry, grind to give you the yeast flour.

To make the brew:

1. Measure a tin of the fermented roasted flour, and pour it into a pot or drum.
2. Add enough water to cover the roasted flour so that the burnt particles can float to the top and be skimmed off. Keep mixing, and drain the water if it is still black, and add more water until you don't have much burnt particles floating on top.
3. Add the ground yeast to the mixture (1 – 1.5 kg yeast) this is where the 'using your heart' bit comes in handy. You just know how much yeast to add depending on the stuff you are using.
4. The next day, the mixture will taste sweet like sugar has been added. This is a sign of a good brew. Mix the brew to make sure

there are no lumps. Add more yeast (1 kg) Add a bit more water, the consistency should be just thick enough to drop off a spoon, not too thick and not too watery. Cover.

5. On the third day, the brew will start bubbling and will start to smell alcoholic. If required mix using a wooden stick and cover.

6. On the fourth day, the brew is ready for drinking. It will taste even better if drunk after 5 to 6 days. And after it has matured, it can keep for a week or two without getting spoilt.

To drink the brew or 'Ajon'

1. Get a clay pot and add the mature 'ajon' in it.

2. Get the tubes for drinking and leave them standing in a container of cold water to soak.

3. Boil water.

4. Add hot water in the pot and using the tube, suck the drink.

5. Absolutely delicious.

6. 'Ajon' is communally drank with people sharing a pot using many straws or tubes.

7. 'Ajon' can also be drank from a calabash or a mug.

NB: never have, eat, or keep any citrus near the 'Ajon' at any stage as the citric acid will spoil it.

Bibliography

1. **Staugthon, John.** 7 amazing benefits of Tamarind. *Organic facts.* [Online] 15 October 2018. [Cited: 19 November 2018.] https://www.organicfacts.net/health-benefits/herbs-and-spices/tamarind.html.

2. *Nutritional Quality and Health Benefits of Okra (Abelmoschus esculentus): A Review.* **HF, Gemede.** 1000458, Nekemte : Journal of Food Processing and Technology, 2015, Vol. 6. 2157-7110.

3. **Ariong, Steven.** Cacabus: A vegetable that makes you thirsty. *Daily Monitor Website.* [Online] 16 July 2012. [Cited: 5 Nov 2018.] http://www.dailymonitor.co.ug/Magazine/Life.

4. **Entin, Beverley.** 7 Benefits of Black-eyde Peas. *NaturalNewsBlogs.* [Online] 12 June 2015. [Cited: 13 November 2018.] https://www.naturalnewsblogs.com/7-health-benefits-black-eyed-peas/.

5. **Nasasira, Roland D.** Health benefits of silver fish. *Daily Monitor.* [Online] 2 January 2018. [Cited: 7 January 2019.] https://www.monitor.co.ug/Magazines/HealthLiving/Health-benefits-of-silver-fish/.

6. **Cebrawski, Katherine.** Furchild Pet Nutrition. *The benefits of offal.* [Online] 30 January 2018. [Cited: 26 February 2019.] https://furchildpets.com/blog/offal/.

7. **Rakhi, Yadama.** Health benefits of finger millet. *Vikaspedia.* [Online] 25 February 2016. [Cited: 10 Oct 2018.]

8. **Brianna, Elliot.** Cassava. *Cassava Wikipedia website.* [Online] 24 March 2017. [Cited: 20 September 2018.] https://www.healthline.com/nutrition/cassava.

Lightning Source UK Ltd.
Milton Keynes UK
UKHW050840160622
404494UK00002B/28